Bone Fragments

Poems by Rick Christiansen

Spartan
Press

Spartan Press
Kansas City, Missouri
spartanpresskc.com

Spartan
Press

Copyright © Rick Christiansen, 2024
First Edition: 1 3 5 7 9 10 8 6 4 2
ISBN: 978-1-958182-61-1
LCCN: 2024930925

Cover and title page image: Helen Miles
Author photo: Rick Christiansen

"Whitman wrote "who touches this book touches a man." When we pick up Rick Christiansen's powerful and elegant *Bone Fragments*, we also touch a man's history and character. The poems are shaped by Christiansen's life, his alcoholic, abusive mother, the younger brother he stole groceries to feed, and now, his relationship with the much-loved grandson he is raising. *Bone Fragments* does not shy away from human beings at their worst—the poems address, unsparingly, neglect and abuse, but Christiansen often holds back from judgment. He understands what it's like not to have options, to do the best you can under the circumstances. In "Baby Teeth," for example, a caregiver prepares to use small pliers to extract a child's recalcitrant baby teeth, dental work that they cannot otherwise afford. The best poetry gives us a sense of the reality of someone else's life, what it's like to be someone else. This is Rick Christiansen's kind of poetry, and if you read *Bone Fragments*, it will be yours as well."

-George Franklin, author of *Remote Cities* and first prize winner of the 2023 W.B. Yeats Poetry Prize.

"A combo of self-fillet and whimsy! Hermann Hesse and Anais Nin on a Tinder date? Swipe right on this book!"

-Frank Higgins, *On Earth as it is* (Spartan Press)

"Rick Christiansen is a gifted writer who knows how to pull you in and keep you reading. His *Bone Fragments* is a fine collection of poems that got under my feet and made me feel a world of emotions. He digs deep, exposes horror, unearths marvels and tugs at the roots of hope and pathos with a penetrating humanity."

-John Burroughs, U.S. National Beat Poet Laureate (2022-23) and author of *Rattle and Numb*

"Rick Christiansen is a poetic archeologist pealing back the layers of his life with no anesthetic. Each transgressive event is dug up and laid out on the white earth of the page for the reader to see. Each poem in this amazing book is a bit of bone from the broken skeleton of his life. *Bone Fragments* opens the poet's life to what must be confronted, must be negotiated, must be accepted, and what must be surrendered, then finally to believe it all and laugh. Christiansen conducts a brilliant, heartfelt and painful excavation of his life. If readers only read one book of poetry this year it should be *Bone Fragments*"

-Walter Bargen, First Poet Laureate of Missouri, author of *Radiation Diary*

"Rick C. Christiansen is a poet whose time has come. His long overdue debut full-length collection *Bone Fragments* is well crafted, heartfelt, and at times almost chillingly honest about the things we all go through in this life, if we live long enough to tell the tale, and thankfully for us, Rick is still out there, his words laid bare on these pages, guiding us home with the truth as his only compass."

-John Dorsey, Author of *Pocatello Wildflower*

In Christiansen's poems, one finds topics as diverse as child abuse; love poems to animals; food insecurity; Alzheimer's. Christiansen shies away from nothing. After reading *Bone Fragments* in its entirety, I realized that, true to the book's title, this is a collection of metaphorical bone fragments drawn from the poet's own rich, complex, (and often quite entertaining) life experiences. Few poets I've read embrace the harshness, the beauty, and the sheer joy of life with the skill and intensity Rick Christiansen displays in this volume."

-D. Ward Hey, Editor, *Stone Poetry Quarterly*

Acknowledgments:

The author would like thank the editors of the following publications where some of these poems first appeared (in some form or another):

"Bone Fragments an archaeological expedition:" *New Generation Beats 2023 Anthology*, "Storm Chasing," "Pig Lung Soup," "Water and Salt:" *The Raven's Perch*, "The Universe Is Porous and Osmosis Creates a Bleeding," "Cardboard Sleds," "Crescent Moon Scars:" *Somewhere Between Kc/Mo And East St. Lou*, "One Shot at a Time," "In London during the War:" *The Rye Whiskey Review*, "Fishsticks:" *PoetryXHunger*, "Baby Teeth," "Sharp Encounters," "Into the Can:" *MacQueen's Quinterly*, "Snow in April:" *Sheila-Na-Gig*, "Blue," "Kites without String," "Tinder Anachronism," "Too Fly," "Eroded Hip Hop Complex:" *Oddball Magazine*, "A Universe of Almost:" *The Literary Parrot*, "George's Bloom:" *Muddy River Poetry Anthology*, "Anarchists in the Kitchen," "Dragging his Beast Around:" *As it Ought to Be Magazine*, "Ode to a Hound Who Is Failing:" *The Dead Pets Poetry Anthology*, "Paradise:" *Into the Fire, Dumpster Fire Press*, "Smoke:" *WINK Magazine*

Table of Contents:

For the friends and teachers who have led me here.

C. Sue Laughran, who over 50 years ago taught me to love words. Maria Nazos, who showed me how to paint with words and Audrey Friedman, who taught me how to wrangle words.

Every step you take is forever. You can't make it go away.
None of it. You understand what I'm sayin?

-Cormac McCarthy,
"No Country for Old Men"

Bone Fragments

An archeological excavation

My mother would disappear, sometimes for up to a
    week. I would
shoplift groceries at the Ralph's in North Hollywood to
    feed my
little brother and myself. It didn't feel like stealing.
    I always took a list.

I don't remember the movie by name. I was 8 or 9.
    I fell hopelessly in
love with the beautiful princess. For the next 50 years,
    I was sure
that I would find her in the bright eyes of every
    neurotic narcissist I dated.
I was always disappointed. But she was always there.

I hate to carry a lot of change in my pockets. It reminds
    me of when I had
to go to the laundromat with my little brother. I always
    tried to use some of
the change to buy him candy. He was easier to handle
    in public spaces when
he had candy.

I was always reluctant to make promises to my children.
I didn't want to disappoint them.
I would just say "we'll see…"
when they asked for a commitment.
They were always disappointed.

1

I killed my dog yesterday. She was failing.
I killed her before she failed. I will never know
when she would have actually failed. I didn't wait
for the end of that movie.

I have built a life around listening to the music others make
and trying to match the syncopation. There is some peace
in slowly going deaf.
                                    It isn't really silence,
just the absence of noise.

More artifacts-another layer

My grandson told me that he thought going to prison
would
be really "awesome"—
He said that it would be relaxing to be forced
into compliance.
Or basically that...

I got $10 an hour to model nude for the art school in
the 1970's.
I told my friends I was doing it for the money.
I was lying.

I tried to become an alcoholic during my Freshman year
of college.
I drank two warm beers for breakfast every
day. But
then I went to class.
I fucked it up.
I should have skipped class.

Last night I dreamed that I shaved off my beard.
My girlfriend broke up with me. Then I woke up.
I told her about the dream and she laughed...
"Yeah, how dare you change your appearance
without my permission!"

My biological mother was 17 when she conceived me.
My daughter was 17 when she conceived my
grandson.

My grandson is now 17.

He lives with me.

I think about what he may be conceiving as I write this.

I lived with my great grandparents

until I was three.

Until my great grandfather

started having seizures.

I asked if he was going to get better.

If I was going to be able to come back

home to them.

They did not want to disappoint me.

They said "we'll see…"

Storm Chasing

The rain pummels the windshield with a force that makes
    it hard to see.
I tighten my hands on the wheel,
my eyes fixed on the wedge shaped cloud in front of me.
I put on my hazard blinkers as I slow down for water on
    the road.
I am not willing to stop.

I am dancing with the elements.
I would chase the clouds on foot if I could…but I am
    slow.
The wind howls and shakes the car. I feel powerful.
I remind myself that I am the pursuer.
I remind myself that I want to be here.

We chase things hoping to be caught. Why else would we?
Proximity creates opportunity.
I want to be in the middle of it all.
I want to swirl through the air.
I want to join the storm

surrounded by cows and surprise.

Into Danger

"All ingenuity is lavished on getting into danger legitimately so that we may be genuinely rescued."
—Robert Frost

I seek the sharp edges, try to find the blind corners.
I wish to be pounced upon.
Running for my life makes my breath stronger.

Needing the darkness as incentive to gulp and flee,
I search and find the right words in my escape.
I do not despair in my search for desperation.

When I am able to find the precipice,
teeter delicately on that ledge,
I find the balance of purpose and the wisdom in
    discomfort.

I relish the startling bump in my night.
I am more awake for its touch.
More alive than when I sit in comfort.

I crash into the sea searching for the waves that will drag
    me deeper.
The sunlight is most lush when it is pursued from the
    depths.
I triumph when I surface and am able to exhale the danger.

I wish for the rope most when I am groping.
If I am able to gain purchase, I hold it with stubborn
    resolve.

My grasp has an unexpected strength.

When I have engineered the rescue, it is always sweeter.
If I am able to extricate others, that is better still.
I will be saved and hero for the circle to complete.

Each action will make us shudder,
Traveling through darkness.
My triumph is in leading us to the light.

The Universe is Porous and Osmosis
Creates a Bleeding

You locked us in our attic bedroom
on nights when you wanted to have sex.

We had to pee in the toy box.
I blamed it on the cat.

We all leak slightly. We all
resist looking at the stain.

At fourteen, I stopped your swinging
stinging slap.

As I caught your wrist in my palm
mid-swing, I saw in your eyes

what you thought you had made.
The punished child becomes

every man who has ever struck you.
Your blows had won, you thought.

I dropped your hand.
I was not your sin eater.

I would not be your sin.

One Shot at a Time

I notice the cars parked askew as I arrive.
Indication of a liquor run, not the first of the day.

They buy their booze one shot at a time.
Tiny airline bottles lined up at the Bodega.

They say they are not alcoholics.
They say—*just one more.*

The eight year old has eighty year old eyes.
He is aging exponentially, one shot at a time.

I teeter on the tight rope.
Balancing love against enablement.

We play a sloppy game of Jenga.
Another shot—to steady the hands.

I see in the eight year old's eyes,
those towers will fall.

I imagine him emerging from the wreckage.
Brushing off the betrayal and disappointment.

One shot at a time.

Fishsticks

Nobody talks about the anger.

Hungry?
Take what you need.
Grab what you want.
Kids laugh at the white paper lunch sack
filled with pilfered snacks from the liquor store.
Slim Jim's…Beef Jerky…Hostess Apple Pie.
"I brought my lunch teacher,
I made it myself."

Nobody talks about the anger.

It was a picnic, wherever they were staying.
The meal arrayed in her lap.
Cold torn bits of sliced wiener
stuck to saltines or sourdough heels.
The children circle her chair
as her chicken hand
dispenses each bite.
Gaping mouths.
Chomp.
Chew.
Swallow.
Take a sip of her Tab cola.

Nobody talks about the anger.

Crash the birthday party in the park.
Blend in—

"I know him from school."

"I forgot to bring my present."

"Is the vegetable platter just for the grownups?"

"Will there be cake?"

"Can I take a piece to my brother?"

Nobody talks about the anger.

At the Dairy Queen—
At the end of the night—
Leftovers go into the dumpster—
It's all still warm—
Sometimes they throw it away in bags—
That makes it easier—

Nobody talks about the anger.

Four Sea King fishsticks—
One slice of Kraft cheese—
A bun if you are lucky—
A packet of tartar sauce—
Snatched from the condiment rack—
At the Seven Eleven—
Taste this Filet-O-Fish—

Nobody talks about the anger.

Rather be hungry than have to be grateful.
Sad doe eyes of observant adults.
Their pity swimming as they try to not feel superior.
Three years old, and I might snatch something off of
    your plate,
even if I don't know you.

Baby Teeth

I just want what is best for him. Lots of reading first, I *am* a nurse. My hands are steady. I know how to set up a sterile field. Clean towels, sterilize the needle nose pliers. Use the small pointy pair—his teeth are small—better for gripping. The dentist said he needs selective extraction so his grown up teeth will come in straight. Lots of reading first. The dentist is right, he *is* telling the truth. He isn't just trying to take my money. The boy *needs* to have it done. It's nobody's fault that we can't afford it. We are self reliant. Lots of reading first, to pick the *right* teeth. He is a good boy. He will sit still for it. It's for his own good. I'll go slow…no…I'll go fast… Like ripping off a bandaid…no…I'll go slow. I have to be careful. I can put down that old plastic tablecloth so no blood gets on the rug. I will set up a sterile field. He will sit still for it. We are partners, a team. It *needs* to be done. Four teeth I think, gotta make room for his big boy teeth. He *is* a big boy. He understands that we have to DO for ourselves. Lots of reading first, to get it right. He will sit still for it. I love him…he *knows* I love him. Some things just need to happen. It's for his own good. He will thank me when his big boy teeth are strong and straight. He will be glad when he smiles at the girls. He will thank me then. Only one tooth to pull each day. He will sit still for it. Four days—four teeth. He can swish some Listerine. We are a team. I will create a sterile field. I can do this. I need to do this. I'll use the little pliers. He has little teeth. He will sit still for it.

Ramblings

We desperately need/
to not need/
each other/
and nobody can do that alone.
It takes a village to flee a town that has stopped being a
    community.

Our faded infrastructure highways have/
the care of the caravan.
Winding away toward
a mountain range
that never seems to grow closer.

It looms in our peripherals/
while we stir the Campbell's
and wish for...one...more...Newport.

Because that first puff in the morning
still tastes like the Sea-and metal/
not metallic...
but the cold steel of a knife in your chest
that can never be coughed all the way up anymore.
And it's not the sea tang
but blood/
and in an hour it *will* be metallic
if it still sits in your gums.

So you swallow.
And/

hope Bill shows up today
cuz you like his dog
and petting her makes you
forget Bill
is there/
and that's good.

Because you never liked that SOB.
But his dog's neck has that kind of fur
that makes you feel like/
you are holding on/
to something real.

Blue Dog

Amnesia fills her mouth,
her history falls away in sheets.
She struggles to speak of acceptance.

One way to control a thing
is to devour it.
Sinning without a plan.

She liked pudding more than ice cream because she
    could
eat it slower.
Now she fears the melt.

Her future self falls into a life of leaving
behind and I watch her through the night.
Dawn is an end.

Like the blue dog with yellow eyes,
she leaves behind
whispers.

When She was Old

If I had seen how waxy her once supple and lustrous
covering had become. Seen her nails, now broken, chipped,
and thorny as I helped to wash her hands—

I would have been able to forgive those hands more
  concretely.

If I had heard her raspy exhalations as she lay her friable
  bones
back onto the pillow and I had cupped her parched neck
  like a cradle while
easing it back onto the pillow more gently than she had
  ever cradled me.

My breath would have come easier.

If I had tucked her in tight under a comforter still warm
  from the dryer.
I would have then been able to look into those
bird bulge eyes/mascara stains that never fade.

Once she looked like an evil starlet.
The one who steals away the good hero
with a switch of her hips and the promise of more.

If I had seen her pelvis, clinging old and closely to her
  thin flannel garment,
I would have seen that once lost girl who had a child
when she was herself still a child.

She had only practiced with dolls. They can take the
    punishment of frustration.
The doll can be thrown aside in impatience.
Limbs left akimbo.

I would not have left her in discomfort.
I would do for her what she should have done for me.
A resurrection found from care.

I would keep the stinging soap from her eyes when I
    washed her hair.
I would not bend the toes painfully when I put on her
    socks.
I would not say hurry through gritted teeth nor bend
    her fingers backwards with a glare of warning.

Her soup would always be warm and not hot.

Her nourishment would not burn going down.

Snow in April

Big lazy unexpected flakes are falling.
The newly bloomed tulips tremble when their cups catch
    the crystals.
She stares out through the glass trying to discern this
    untimely tableau.

She knows she has vascular dementia.
But she still has a very full life.
She talks to people all day long.

But the hallucinations are intractable.
She cannot trust that her chatting partner is not smoke.
Still, one-sided dialogue is underrated.

She surprises herself with her secrets.
She needs this play of conversation to find her shifting
    boundaries
before they impinge and impact others in ways that she
    does not intend.

It is like that with this snow.
She asks herself if she should mention it.
She knows that they are planning to install the 5G soon.

She hopes that will improve her reception.
She hates to have to ask for things to be repeated.
If she tells about the snow they might move her down
    on the list.

It is starting to accumulate on the grass and the blooms
    are bending from the weight.
With shifting clarity and confusion
she remembers an NPR story about global warming.

She still remembers about the calories.
It makes her sad to remember enough
to know that she cannot always remember.

She decides to keep her own counsel.
The snow will certainly melt.
And the tulips will be unbowed when the weight of
    white cover has been lifted.

Hands

I asked my mother once, after my father had died, what her favorite thing about him had been. She sat and thought for a long moment. I watched the muscles of her face move as she considered the question. I knew her face. I could discern even shadows of emotion as she shifted expressions. She, at first looked thoughtful, then wistful and finally a look of satisfaction settled in her gaze. *"His hands,"* she said gently. I waited for her to say more. But her declaration had carried her inside of herself for a moment. Finally, she spoke.

"After the cancer and the mastectomy the nurse had to give us detailed care instructions for the wound where my breast had been removed. There was a small tube sutured into the incision that extended out almost an inch. The nurse called it a drain. All of this had to be cleaned and re-bandaged each day. It was not something I could do alone. Your father listened carefully to all of the instructions and watched the nurse dress the site with the gauze and bandages. I was not able to make myself even look down to where my breast had been as she worked. I just looked at your father. Then we drove home.

That night, it was time to clean and redress the incision and drain. Your Dad didn't say anything. He just set out the bandages and gauze and other supplies on a tv tray he had placed next to the high back chair he had put near our bed. He led me to the chair and helped me sit down. He sat directly in front of me on a lower chair that positioned his face in front of my chest. I remember his hands. So large and rough from the garden, gently and almost delicately unbuttoning the front of my nightgown and removing the dressing from my chest. I would not look down. I felt the air where my breast should be.

Your father's expression never changed as he worked. It was the same look he had on his face when he put finishing touches on one of his paintings. I focused on looking at his hands. I remember being SO frightened that he would pull back or be disgusted by my hollow chest with a tube protruding. I can talk about it now. His face was only inches from my deformity. His hands worked gently but firmly. Feeling his hands on me...reassured me...I think...I imagined him painting something beautiful. I always loved his hands."

Blue

My blue is not like your blue.

You may be moved by a sky or an ocean.

I reside in the azure stare of a small blond monarch.

20 pounds.

Smaller than a bag of groceries.

Feet planted firmly in response to a frame that still
wavers.

Gamboling into instant mood shifts.

Ruler of all she surveys.

Nimble fingers in sticky explorations to distinguish the
world from self.

So anxious, this blue, to make all new things become
old and familiar.

From discovery to understanding in an instant.

The dog becomes her steed.

A reluctant gallop from beneath her spell.

Joy in creating. Satisfaction in destruction.

Each day a mountainous fraction of a lifetime.

Always the little sister.

Delighted conquest without regard for consequences.

Be ready, there may be blood.

Cardboard Sleds

I watch the children turn our summer hill into winter
   again.
They ride their cardboard boxes down our mound of
   sun-scorched grass.

I sit in my chair on the patio and swallow their joy.
The wonder in grass as snow and a sleigh ride
in shorts and a tee shirt.

The incongruity makes me smile
and elicits pealing giggles from these young souls.

Silly hill! Who knew that you could wear so many
   different coats?
Sliding through seasons and staying true to your
   childish purpose.
Slippery grass shining in the sun like the crystals of a
   frosty morning.

The children swerve down the elevation with abandon.
The climb back up is easier without the snow.

Legs languid in the heat.
Climbing the incline again and again.
Turning our slope into a sweaty mountain.

With each descending cascade the grass surrenders
   more dust.
As twilight approaches I finally call in the tumbling herd.

Miss Firecracker 1964

She liked the way the guys at the firehouse looked at her,
when she walked by pushing the stroller with a toddler
   in hand.
They didn't even see the kids.

They saw Miss Firecracker 1964.
High ass and long legs and just a hint of swish
in her step and sashay.

She had to take the long way to the store,
to go by the firehouse when she needed milk.
But the exercise was good for her.

She liked the feel of their eyes on her,
when she got to the long driveway where they washed
   the trucks.
She always remembered to slow down just a little bit.

Sometimes she stopped the stroller right in front.
Bending over the baby, back to the trucks, backside on
   display,
pretending to fuss over one of the kids. Just for the
   attention, no harm done.

She had always intended to be more than what she had
   become.
That high ass and long legs
were gonna be her ticket out of town.

Maybe it wasn't too late.
Cuz she still had it!
Even after pushing out the brats.

Because they sure did stop and look
when she stopped for the looking.
Miss Firecracker 1964.

Twirling a toddler now, not a baton.
But she still looked good.
She never ate dessert and walking everywhere helped.

She was gonna go to beauty school.
Get good at making everybody else
look almost as good as her.

But she liked it when he showed her how he felt.
Instead of just telling her.
And that kind of conversation makes babies.
And now she has two kids.
And he doesn't show her, or tell her anymore.
So she walks the long way past the firehouse.

Miss Firecracker 1964 *Redux*

I liked the way the guys at the firehouse looked at me.
When I walked by pushing the stroller with a toddler in
    hand.
They didn't even see the kids.

They saw Miss Firecracker 1964.
High ass and long legs,
and just a hint of swish in my step and sashay.

I had to take the long way to the store,
to go by the firehouse when I needed milk.
But the exercise was good for me.

I liked the feel of their eyes on me,
when I got to the long driveway
where they washed the trucks.

I always remembered to slow down
just a little bit. Sometimes,
I stopped the stroller right in front.

Bending over the baby,
back to the trucks, backside on display,
pretending to fuss over one of the kids.

Just for the attention, no harm done.
I had always intended to be
more than what I had become.

That high ass and long legs
were gonna be my ticket
out of town.

Maybe it wasn't too late.
Cuz I still had it!
Even after pushing out the brats.

Because they sure did stop and look when I stopped
    for the looking.
Miss Firecracker 1964. Twirling a toddler now, not a
    baton.
But I still looked good.

I never ate dessert and walking everywhere helped—
I was gonna go to beauty school.
Get good at making everybody else look *almost* as
    good as me.

But, I liked it when he showed me how he felt,
instead of just telling me.
And that kind of conversation makes babies.

And now I have two kids.
And he doesn't show me, or tell me anymore.
So I walk the long way past the firehouse.

A Universe of Almost

We spend the first half of our lives accumulating.
It is a season for gathering, a time to pack the pantry.
In the second half we must reconcile accounts.

What has been gathered will be returned.
The debt will be repaid.
I will pay my debt with words.

Joy must be manufactured.
It is a cottage industry.
We mold happiness like a new clay pot,
fashioned within the circle of our arms.

There is strength in acceptance.
Sometimes we must swallow without question.

We are survivors in this forest.
Like a fern living amongst the tree roots,
we make our peace with any soil.

I tell myself to be as grateful as the circumstances of my
    life deserve.
That I have the voice I have been given.
That it is important for me to sing.

But it is easier to just be clever.
To build a stackable life.
To reside in a Universe of almost.

But, I do not want to be left like the biblical Job.
Rending his garments in the ashes and asking…why?
I encourage myself to fold the ash into the earth and
     plant again.

So each morning when I am fresh and still in my robe,
with my dog and my coffee beside me. I will write what
     I know.

Then, I will read aloud what I have written
and throw punctuation at it
like darts in a carnival midway game.

Interstate

Highway 70
Cascading like the river
Taking us all home

Cross the Missouri
Again and again winding
Looking at each shore

Corn on one side now
Soybeans always adjacent
Monsanto rules

Tornado alley
Rapid temperature change
Finding your haven

Beer, bait and bullets
Holy trinity sale
What more is needed?

Two coasts this state
No ocean on either shore
Yet still an island

Sharp Encounters

Haibun

The butcher had only one hand. I would watch him make the steaks and chops. He would place the meat on the block carefully. Arranging it so as to make the intended entry point of the blade most accessible. He would then pick up the knife or cleaver and slice or chop in a single motion. He would next lay down the implement and again arrange the meat for a cut. Again and again he would repeat these movements until he had enough for the platter he placed each day in the window of the shop. I think he lost the hand in the war. But, who knows. He was a butcher. So many sharp encounters.

the door is open
I hope you can see it now
that is all I want

Traces

Haibun

The taint of loss is like a dormant ache, awakening as
I hold these photographs. I wonder where she is now,
what paths she's walked, and if she, too, gazes at these
same faded images, feeling the weight of time's passage.
I rub the slick Polaroids with my thumb. Willing back my
history.

In soil's secret keep
Blooms in silence bound

Into the Can

Haibun

The small black kitten has been crushed, not yet quite
dead. Her dark eyes are slits in her flattened face. Her
white teeth are showing through her opened mouth,
the tip of her pink tongue rests on the teeth, slightly
protruding. She is trembling with small convulsions. I
hold her in my 10 year old hands, ask my stepfather,
almost pleading, if we can take her to the doctor.
"No point," he says. *"She's trash now, put her in the
can outside."* I walk up the steps from our basement
apartment cradling the kitten in my upturned palms. I
can still feel her trembling. I reach the heavy gray metal
trash can. With the kitten in the crook of one arm, I pry
off the frozen lid. I place the kitten onto the mound
of cardboard and garbage in the can. It is twilight. Her
black form lays on its side on the cardboard, like a
charcoal cameo. I slowly replace the lid.

some need to grow thorns
to touch the pearl drop waters
part of me falls through

Epistemology

Haibun

RAPE-

We didn't think about that word for what happened. It felt
more like a punishment. Something to be endured. He was
only 10. Drawn into an alcove. I was never clear on the
enticement. I was 14. I chose not to press. I am now 65.
I imagine my current self, comforting this little brother.
I feel more equipped. God…of course I do. But still
insufficient. Good only to bear witness. Finding the dignity
in circumstance. How does a child do this?

Owl's eyes pierce through snow's veil
But still a forest

Pig Lung Soup

Generations survive by turning waste into delicacy

I remember
Many times
In the back seat of a car
Holding my whole world
In a paper bag
In my lap
No idea where
We were going
Just knowing
We had to get away
From where we were

The day comes
You look at your parent
A childish realization
They are lost
You do not have a net

You begin to fold
And refold
Creating layers of protection
Nothing but skin and innocence

You must explore
This new country
In which you now live

You must become
More pragmatic
Than devout
Rub your own hope
Into your face
With the dry heels of your small hands

There is no vacation
From the irrational vigilance
That has no object
And grants no power

You trade away intimacy
For control

And it comes

You navigate
The jagged rocks
A world that would benefit
From hands that would do better to be idle

And it comes

A faint chant
Rising in volume
A sound devoid of pity

And it comes

Finding residual illumination
From the refuse you are granted

Finding warmth in the friction of relationships
Built past the childhood taken

In the end
Everything must be chewed and digested.

Crescent Moon Scars

I still see the vague echo of scars
on the inside of my forearm
where she gripped me
—her brightly colored nails
—biting into the flesh.

It is a form of love to want to control something
—no matter what the cost.

"Sit still and shut up!"

She needed me to do that
so her attention could focus
—on whatever man was the latest
—and ripe for the picking.

We were a team
—she would say
—harvesting the next meal ticket.

I hoped each man
and each scar
might earn me back
my bicycle.

Left in a storage bin
—near Bakersfield
—or maybe Riverside.

When we again sped the Mustang
—pell mell across the desert.
To a new place
where her face would also be new
and her stories would be believed.

Bone On Bone

Party of the first part—

I vaguely remember her childhood.
Something gooey
and some Tinker Toys.

She is bitter.
She perceives the benefits wrought
from competence, as luck— in others.

A buffet of dysfunction
kept warm by a heat lamp
of anxiety.

The memories feel
both heavy and light
in my pocket.

We thought her tantrums
were only mascara
and puffery.

I tried to experience her anger
as a transitional phase
of her development.

But she made it hard.
Going instinctively and
straight to the softest meat.

Selfishness and
survival are often
the same thing.

Party of the second part—

I am looking for that string in my gullet.
Fishing with wet fingers to gain purchase
sufficient to pull up new resolve into the air.

I have lost the dichotomy needed.
Blame and responsibility are
eroded by the friction of use.

A spectacular failure has its grace.
An end is defined and closed.
This seesaw of recovery is exhausting.

The entropy of family.
The mingling of guilt and intent.
I want to activate the mechanism of flight.

I can hear my history.
I see those ghosts who once exhaled steps
along these same pitted hallways.

What made this so?
Genetic lysosomes? Suicide sacs of inevitability?
But, I must not be dragged south by the corpse of past
    tense.

It would be too precious to rest this all

on ancient shoulders. The load
must be present for ownership.

Still, I feel weighed down by
the fossils that I carry.
My life is painted by rust.

We are all similar enough.
The wrists of each generation
pass through the same stained sleeves.

Still, I have ambition for her recovery.
I listen for the scratch of her shovel in the dirt.
She must snatch back her own choices from our Elysian
    Fields.

I remember, they are not mine.
I must untangle.
I am ignoring my dusting.

George's Bloom

The bad stuff never stops happening really. It fades for
    awhile
And then re-emerges as prophecy. We learn that about
    memory.
Experience cuts deep lines into the self.

Families are like storms. They can rumble and darken for
    awhile.
And then the rain starts. Sometimes there is lightening
    and you hope for shelter.
Because it can steal your breath away and cause third degree
    burns.

You may wish that it was all more like a game of Checkers.
A board you could pull out only when you wished. A set
    number of pieces
Half one shade and half another. Always assembled in
    the same configuration
With unchanging rules and predictable outcomes.

But instead you have to listen for the wind. Sniff the air.
    Watch the clouds.
Sometimes you have to hurry home.

We lost George a couple of years ago. But he is still
    somehow present.
I do not hear his voice. It is hard to explain. I sense his
    intent.
He urges me towards patience and acceptance as I prepare
    for each coming storm.

I do not hear his voice.
But I feel the words. I feel more than the words
I feel the meaning of those words and their importance.
It is conveyed to me daily and most strongly when the
     wind has risen
And I can smell how deep the rain is going to be.

Patience and acceptance.
Almost like a Yoga coach whispering behind your right ear.
"Breathe."

The experience is figurative, not literal.
But it is him.

Soon after George was gone away from us in all of the
Ways and manners in which most people mark departure,
I was looking at a yard full of identical bushes.
Each bush was covered by green tinged blossoms.
But there was one blossom that bucked the trend.
A flower going its own way. It was brilliantly white and
     seemed to surge forward
Away from all the rest. It was unexpectedly unique.

I knew that it would fade and wilt and that, over time,
     new storms would scatter its' petals.
But I hoped for it to re-emerge as prophecy.
And it has.
Patience and acceptance.
George's Bloom.

Kites without string

At first you ran
looking behind you to gauge loft and direction.
Hopeful that the trajectory you had chosen
would result in untangled flight for what you have
    launched.
Aspiring to heights where the horizon curves into
    infinity.
Watching buffeting wind lift its' charge to soar without
    firm destination.
Random air giving altitude and vantage for detecting
whispers of other landscapes.
This awareness creating a thirst which overwhelms
the need for attachment. The string becoming an
    unnecessary
artifact of control.
You know that to harvest, a fruit must be released from
    its' stem.
But you hope it will still be grounded.
Still have a tail pointing toward its' origin.
You know that not all fledglings fly from the nest.
Some simply drop.
Destined to nourish the boughs that shelter siblings
    and generations.
Geese have been observed reacting to such a death by
    flying and calling,
Searching until they themselves become disoriented
    and lost.
It is a risk to untether
and to be untethered.

Anarchists in the Kitchen

We searched for the can opener in all the usual places.

His rueful stare, when I unearthed a small Flintstone's
    jelly glass,
half full of expired lime-flavored Alka-Seltzer tablets—
and the way he stitched his breath—when
he was thinking—alerted me to attend and wait
for his next thought
before opening the next drawer.

I noticed that the Flintstone glass was a rare one, with a
    faded and flaking image of Dino on it.
"Dino always freaked me out!", he said,
"I felt that having a dinosaur as a pet would be a
    crushing responsibility."

I nodded and kept looking through drawers.

He watched me search as he plucked absently at the hair
    on his cheek.
I was running out of drawers and still no can opener.

He had the look of a visiting shaman,
who knows that
he must serve as a reluctant muse.

"We are going to have to rethink this."
He said.

I knew he had a gift for climbing inside of things and
    pushing outward.

I waited.

He held up a wonderful old corroded French chef's
    knife triumphantly.
I remembered that it had belonged to my aunt.
Who had gotten it from her brother, salvaged from the
    ashes
of an old hotel kitchen fire.

"We will open the cans with this", he said.

He popped the point of the knife
into the first can, and began to saw and pry his way
    around the rim.

"See…we are anarchists", he said.
I pointed out that this was an old Boy Scout camping
    trick.

And he responded,
"Exactly."

Dragging His Beast Around

The habit was structured, controlled, modulated—
Architecture married to inspiration.
Never too much—it was always too much.
Gone in a stutter.

Chasing God.
You were not supposed to catch up.
The cliché too painful.
No choice but to be seen.

There is risk in being seen.
Beast seeping out by inches.
Like yellow jackets oozing
from the nest.

You didn't *have* to wait until life
was *not* hard to be happy.
You were going to outlast
the buzz and swarming.

Two coasts—your face.
No ocean on either shore,
yet still an island.
Made lethargic by the needle.

You circled a thing that wasn't there
until you forced it into existence.
Belief leaks when you chase chaos.
And you can get caught up short.

Low Rider

She's a low rider – chassis almost touches the ground
Ears that sweep a path before her like Moses parts the sea
White tipped tail telegraphs her trajectory
She weaves through scents without sense
Nose to the ground
Learning more from a blade of grass
Than the contents of a dictionary

She slips the bounds of her boundaries
Brimming with a belly bouncing on the ground
Hungry for the promise of the next trail
Straining at the lead
Force enough for dislocation
Taking corners like an Indy car
Hound enough for herself

She talks me into one more trail
Both chests heaving
Both tongues hanging
Both butts dragging
Chase without prey
Rabid for the rabbit
Hound enough for us both

She's a low rider —chassis now touching the ground
Past the porch we pace
Foam speckles the air
She shakes her folds for one more round
Still straining at the lead

Sniffing at phantom beasts
Hound enough for us all

Hound enough for us all

Ode to a Hound who is Failing

First—
She is a *who*, not a *what*—personality manifest
stubbornness and affection. A spirit soft and malleable
as her long velvet ears.

Grunts as a pup evolved into the groans of age.
Neither a complaint, both an assertion of effort
born from instinct, honed by character.
Life is a target.

Like chasing a rabbit on the run, everything
is focused on the try. I watch her hips
waver climbing the stairs. An errant foot
cascading to the side and then:

recovery of balance that reclaims dignity.
She is not mournful, only determined
to remain herself through the entropy.
Cataract squint across the room to see

what has already been discerned by
a nose that will NEVER fail. More groans
to rise and greet, as the lady of the manor,
all those who come to her home.

She is always welcoming—accepting
of all that join her space. Her hunting
mellowed to a search for friends.
Magnanimous instinct no more discerning prey.

I think she knows that *she* is now hunted.
Age overtakes her once swift stride and
ambles beside her. Ready to strike—
I hope death is patient as I am not ready.

She is ready for anything that comes.
A lifetime of calm acceptance—she will
accept her last visitor as she has greeted
everyone before: with gentle attention.

Tinder Anachronism

I imagine Hermann Hesse and Anaïs Nin
Both swiping right
They would meet in a small Paris coffee bar
Anaïs would flick the whip cream from her cup
Using just the tip of her tongue as punctuation
Hermann would watch her carefully
And finger the Nobel he wears as a cravat
Clearing his throat nervously
He would talk quietly about the First Great War
By the second cup
They would be dishing on Henry Miller
But not about June
And saying that to be an artist requires
An income
Or resourcefulness
Or both
Hermann would remark upon her narrow calf skin boots
And tell her
That they look very smart and smooth
Anaïs would tilt her head and smile
Thinking of other older men she has tasted
And with her eyes she would swipe right again
And Hermann would see the glance
And nod
And pay the check
As he tells her about the balcony
And the cat
In the apartment he has borrowed
Just around the corner

Paradise

I imagine Lawrence Ferlinghetti
And Mark Rothko meeting
As they dumpster dive
Together in the ether
Each drawn there
By the same smell of rancid chicken
But for very different reasons
Mark could help Larry
Up and into the container
Age before beauty after all
They would both smirk
And they would get their hands dirty
Because that is what you do when you make something
    worthwhile
It is never too late to create something
that people are NOT ready to see.

Smoke

A love story

She was
Of all things
Quick
She would waver and

Slip from focus
Object and spectator
Blurred speed concealing
Reason diminishing

Line and distance
Close at once
Then receding into
Relief

In her domicile
Another cigarette
To distract I am not
A distraction

Distraction
Can be
Captured
By tar smoke and even

Breath
I loom into the consciousness neither flat nor
Quick I am not
Afraid of smoke

To Fly

I do not wish

I have soared through treetops stretching sinew and
    bone.
Feeling the movement of the ocean's air with
    it's tang and promise of...
Avoiding branches by millimeters.
Making the trees hum with intention.

Now I will sit, not truly resting
Waiting...waiting…
Things that certainly will
Come anticipating what
May not, prepared none
The less.

Is this truly a cage if I choose to remain within its'
    comforting bars?

My perch a throne from which to contemplate
All things, but
Participate?

Is.
This
Rest?
This memory of flight animates my nerves.
Makes ME hum like the trees. I feel
As rooted, nourished

My silent assent to what
May come...
Still waiting...
Breathing through
My fear clutching
With talons for vantage and
Courage.
Outside

Others see to my needs.
Sustenance without understanding
Trust without knowledge

Signaling scattered head
Bobs a constant
Stare
My potential released into the infinite
Space containing
My finite
Wish

Eroded Hip Hop Complex

I.

KRUNK!

Say the dust motes falling into the sunlight before me.

An act of becoming and dissolving.
Our death is our wedding with these things.

I feel it in the firmness of each footstep taken.
And myself, in the lifting of that step.

The artisan searches for what is not there
In order to practice his craft.

I practice stillness in my movement.
I am not there.

II.

KRUNK!

Say the joints that ache while they dance through the floor.

Anxiety makes ME warm.
And so, I contribute to the process.

I make trinkets to prove that I exist.
I display them to force their existence.

Even tea will intoxicate.
If only you drink it quickly.

The body will nurture the mind and provide
Bad advisement.

III.

KRUNK!

Say the utensils that I have laid down after their use.

I am much too small a place to live.
I must stretch and groan into fullness.

I have pulled my own existence out of this fissure.
I have not forgotten the traces of my gifts.

I remember the poverty of emptiness.
I will not travel there again.

The flavor of optimism builds on my tongue.
And I swallow.

Prescription

The doctor told my great grandfather that my great
  grandmother
should have a glass of wine before dinner each evening.

Good to replenish her iron—and she was a nervous sort,
  although
no one ever really talked about that in more than vague
  terms.

Papa wanted Momma to be just right.
They were not drinkers…but the doctor said…

Papa bought a big green bottle of Chianti—
the kind nestled in a woven grass basket.

Momma always listened to Papa.
Papa always listened to the doctor.

She drank her wine. The whole glass, everyday.
A week passed—

Papa didn't understand, Momma was following doctor's
  orders.
But, she had stopped cooking dinner. She just fell asleep—

In her chair with the pro wrestling in the background.
On the flickering TV.

Papa wanted Momma to be just right. He called the

doctor. Told him
Momma was sleeping away dinner. Woke with a
    headache each morning.

The doctor still made house calls. He came to the house
and asked to see the wine…and the glass…

Papa dutifully fetched the Chianti—
And the 16 ounce tumbler glass.

He filled it to the brim. *See doctor—*
we follow your prescription! The doctor hid his smile.

The next day the doctor returned with a gift.
Two wine glasses in a box. The doctor told Papa…

Only one of these each day—
and not filled to the brim.

Momma made pork chops and potatoes for dinner.

In London during the War

In London during the War—
The sound of dripping syrup methodically tapping a
    tattoo on the shelf below,
from a can of peaches pierced by bomb shrapnel
while sitting on a London apartment shelf
during the blitz.

In our plague year—
The sound of an ICU respirator
wheezing to a stop
after the code has been called.
Time of death marked by the patient's cell phone
now unplugged and placed in the bag for her children.

This Plague year has changed us all.
Time speeding up and slowing down to the rhythms of
    serotonin.
Anxiety creating brilliant, focused experience,
like a microscope being dialed in to the cellular level.

They say that in London during the war,
people felt more alive.
The Spector of sudden death from the sky
made them love faster, drink longer, fuck harder.

In our Plague year—
We endure the Spector of slow death.
Not from the sky, but from the air.

Droplets like shrapnel piercing the lungs/slowly
        stealing breath away.
We only grow heavier.
Eating and watching and hiding from the miasma.

They say that in London during the War,
people died alone trapped in the wreckage of bombed
        buildings.

In our Plague year—
people die alone trapped in hospital beds.
Tethered to machines instead of family.
Each breath more shallow than the last, until the
        ragged sound stops.

They say that in London during the War,
each morning people would emerge blinking.
Wearing masks against the dust and smoke.
Marking the demise of another shop or restaurant to
        bomb or fire
as they navigated the minimums of life.

Picking up a prescription.
Trying to find milk or toilet paper.

Because children are still thirsty
and we must shit until we die.

Wandering for items that would fill the hole
of uncertainty and named fear.

The anonymity of masked travel.

Making the eyes do all of the work of the face.
Trying to connect through fabric and fear.

In our Plague year—
It is the same.

They say that in London during the War,
everyone pulled together.
They had the connection of a shared enemy.

In our Plague year—
we are denied that connection.
False news and finger pointing make us misdirect our
    resolve
away from shared purpose.
Toward disconnecting conspiracy and suspicion.

They say that in London during the War,
Everyone became stronger.

In our Plague year—

Water and Salt

I feel a need of cleansing.
Briskness against my palate to scrub this year away.
I imagine a scoured veneer where hope will again find
    adhesion.

Like a wooden planked deck, stained by time and life,
made fresh with a stiff brush doused in water
and drawn across a salted surface.

My spirit craves this reckoning with the elements.
These artifacts of baptism providing me too with
    renewal.
Both ingredients of the sea. Washing over me almost
    battering.

Too much dust has settled on my sensibilities.
Solitude and uncertainty have soiled my gaze.
I will start again in water and salt.

Lists

I learned from my father
that a good man leaves behind
unfinished lists.

Milk
Cookies
Ice cream
Fruit
Buy graph paper

My lists have changed,
since you came to live with me.
They will change again.

You are shifting daily in the way that young things do.
I had forgotten this speed of transformation.
I have been focused on my own entropy.

Look at me raising a colt again.
Look at you learning to jump fences.
Look at us both adjusting our pace, so that we can walk
    together.

Cereal (he likes the sweet ones)
Rice
Pick him up after tutoring (3:00 PM)
Mexican style cheese
Pay the High School Wood Shop fee — ($30.00)

Your abrupt residence here is startling to me.
I expected quiet years toward an inevitable end.
Instead, I have a roommate.

A gangling puppy in blue jeans and a hoodie.
Feet and hands too large,
a voice deepening and no longer crackling.

I make my inventories so that we will both have
    structure,
an order to our unexpected days together.
You never write anything down.

Youth believes that if it is truly important—it will be
    remembered.
Age knows that words on paper—are real,
a promise.

I will catalogue what we both will need.
I will keep writing it all down.
You too, will begin to compose.

Together we will cross off the items,
marking the progression
of this parade from page to life.

Words Float

My Dad said that
when he was gone
he wanted to leave a hole.

He is gone.

His wish was granted and there is a hole.

Now I fill that hole with words.
Every few days I drop some in
and watch them descend into the pile.

Nouns seem to weigh more
and they sink down past the surface layer.
Displacing verbs and bumping aside adjectives..

The hole is recently filling with water.
Perhaps there is a subterranean spring
or, run off from the Spring rains.

No matter.

Words can float.
Bob on the surface.
Bounce into one another creating patterns in the water.

Sometimes they submerge from their own weight.
And leave only a small peak above the water line.
Like an iceberg, hiding their true volume under the
    rippling surface.

Some words sit atop others and become swollen from
    the moisture.
It would be trite to imagine that some of that moisture
could be tears — or whiskey.

That word pile has already been written.

I try to do more than just stack the words
If I did— of course it could fall.
That is physics.

But the art of dropping prepositions from above.
Hoping they land where intended.
And then rebuilding when they do not.

That is an art and a meditation.

I imagine my father experiencing the hole
he has left.
Slowly filling with my words.

I hope that he is feeling comfortably full.

Rick Christiansen is a former corporate executive, stand-up comedian, actor and director. His work can be found in *MacQueen's Quinterly, Oddball Magazine, Stone Poetry Journal, The Rye Whiskey Review, As It Ought to Be Magazine* and other publications. His poem "BONE FRAGMENTS' is included in the 2023 *New Generation Beats Anthology* from the National Beat Poetry Foundation. He has been recently nominated for a Touchstone Award. He is the co-host of SpoFest, a member of The Writer's Place and a member of The St. Louis Writers Guild. He lives in Missouri near his fiancé Kim and his eight grandchildren.

This project was made possible, in part, by generous support from the Osage Arts Community.

Osage Arts Community provides temporary time, space and support for the creation of new artistic works in a retreat format, serving creative people of all kinds — visual artists, composers, poets, fiction and nonfiction writers. Located on a 152-acre farm in an isolated rural mountainside setting in Central Missouri and bordered by ¾ of a mile of the Gasconade River, OAC provides residencies to those working alone, as well as welcoming collaborative teams, offering living space and workspace in a country environment to emerging and mid-career artists. For more information, visit us at www.osageac.org

Osage Arts Community